The giant liked stories about dwarves.

The dwarves liked stories
about princesses.

The princess liked stories about princes.

And when the prince got sleepy,

he liked bedtime stories most of all!

Edmonton, 48" × 48", Oil on Linen, RFM McInnis

F

Frank Slide

The Frank Slide took place in the Crowsnest Pass on 29 April 1903. It was one of the biggest rockslides of historic times. In 1900 S.W. Gebo arrived looking for coal deposits to mine and located here. The following year A.L. Frank, from Butte, Montana, helped Gebo develop his mine. They formed the Canadian American Company. Soon a town was built up around the Turtle Mountain mine. The town officially opened on 10 September 1901. When the mountain roared down on the sleeping people a year and a half later, it killed seventy, and largely destroyed the town. You can still see Frank Lake, which was formed by the slide.

Today the little community of Frank is peaceful and quiet. But look closely at the painting. You can see where the side of Turtle Mountain slid down and destroyed the town.

Frank Slide, 20" × 20", Oil on Linen, RFM McInnis

G

Grande Prairie

Grande Prairie is a descriptive name. The Cree gave the area a name meaning "big prairie". The first mention of the name was included in the Hudson's Bay Company's Fort Dunvegan post journal in 1854. As with most descriptive names there were other names for the area. The Northwest Company traders called the grand prairie the Buffalo Plains. Many places could receive the same name. Today Grande Prairie is the name of a city, a county, a creek, and the large open prairie itself.

Grande Prairie is ideal country for farming and has attracted agricultural settlement since the first trails and railways allowed access to the northern districts. Farm auctions are an important part of rural life. In this painting hundreds of neighbours gather for an auction.

Grande Prairie, 16" × 20", Oil on Linen, RFM McInnis

H Head Smashed In

Head Smashed In buffalo jump is a natural place where bison could be lured or driven over a cliff to be killed by First Nations hunters. Many buffalo jumps are located across the plains in Canada and the United States. This was one of the biggest buffalo jumps in Alberta. Today it is a World Heritage Site because of what it can tell us about how people lived before Europeans came.

The Blackfoot name for this site is estipah-skikikini-kots. This name means "where he got his head smashed in." This does not refer to bison. It comes from a Peigan legend that tells how a young Peigan man wanted to see the buffalo crashing to the bottom of the cliff. He took shelter at the foot of the jump before they were driven over. The bison fell so fast, and there were so many of them, that they covered him and crushed him to death.

Head Smashed In has been an important site for First Nations people for many years. It was an important area for harvesting the buffalo for thousands of years. People gather here for a Pow Wow, a cultural celebration.

Head Smashed In, 16" × 20", Oil on Linen, RFM McInnis

I

Innisfail

This name reminds us that sometimes we do not really know the origin of a place-name. In one account, Innisfail appears to have been named for a place in Argyllshire, Scotland. Another story tells us that it was named for the Irish homeland of the grandmother of Estella Scarlett, an early resident of Innisfail. The Gaelic name Innis Vail refers to Ireland, and means Isle of Destiny.

The first name for this town was Poplar Grove. Many of the first place-names were descriptive, but later settlers changed them to reflect their attachment to their home countries or cultures.

Innisfail, 16" × 20", Oil on Linen, RFM McInnis

J

Jasper

The name Jasper originated with the fur trade. In about 1813 the Northwest Company of fur traders built a trading post or "house" at Brule Lake. Later it was moved to be near to Jasper Lake. First known as Rocky Mountain House, this post was renamed Jasper House for Jasper Hawse, the trader in charge at the second location. The Hudson's Bay Company took over the post, but stopped using it in 1884. When the Grand Trunk Pacific Railway built through the area it set up its divisional point and called it Fitzhugh, for a prominent company man. But when Jasper Park was named in 1907, the town name gradually changed to be the same as that of the park. Today there is a park, town and lake named Jasper.

James Simpkins, a cartoonist, created Jasper the Bear for *Maclean's* Magazine. The cartoon was popular from 1949 to 1969, and again from 1971 to 1975. The bear's antics amused generations of Canadian readers, and Jasper was embraced by the town that gave him his name. Today Jasper greets travelers at the railway station.

Jasper, 16" × 20", Oil on Linen, RFM McInnis

K

Kootenay Plains

Sir James Hector visited the Kootenay Plains in 1858. He was exploring for the famous Palliser Expedition, hoping to discover valuable resources in the unexplored western lands. Dr. Hector wrote in his journal that the place already had this name when he arrived. The Kootenai people used to exchange furs here with traders from the trading posts along the Saskatchewan River tributaries. A yearly gathering was held in these plains for years.

The Kootenay Plains have a climate that makes them a special place. They are dry and relatively warm. Kootenai people crossed the mountains to the west to trade and hunt bison because of these features. Today the area is an important ecological region where you can find sand dunes, calcium rich wetlands, limber pine and grasslands.

Kootenay Plain, 16" × 20", Oil on Linen, RFM McInnis

L

Lake Louise

This lake is one of the best-known places in Alberta among the many thousands of travelers from around the world who stay at the Chateau Lake Louise.

This lake has had several names. Such re-naming of places has often been the case in Alberta. Tom Wilson, the famous guide and outfitter, called this lake Emerald Lake when he first saw it in 1882. Before him, the Stoney people called it the Lake of Little Fishes. On a second look, in 1884, Wilson decided the lake was blue, not emerald, and renamed it Louise, after the daughter of a man who was traveling with him. The official name, however, was for another "Louise." The CPR was beginning to promote tourism to the area at the time. The company decreed that the lake would be named to honour Her Royal Highness Princess Louise Caroline Alberta, the fourth daughter of Queen Victoria. The Province of Alberta also was named for her.

Lake Louise, 20" × 20", Oil on Linen, RFM McInnis

M

Medicine Hat

Medicine Hat is likely the most famous place name in Alberta. The old Blackfoot name meant "head-dress of a medicine man." There are several stories about how the name came about. One tells how a fight between Cree and Blackfoot warriors took place. In the fighting a Cree chief lost his headdress in the river. There is also a hill located east of Medicine Hat which looks like a headdress. This hill was given that name on a map in 1883. So perhaps the town took its name from this physical feature. In 1907 Rudyard Kipling visited the city and called it "the city with All Hell for a basement" because of the tremendous natural gas reserves located there. Kipling said of the name: "It has no duplicate in the world; it makes men ask questions...." In 1910 the people of Medicine Hat were considering a new name, more appropriate for a bustling city. Rudyard Kipling was among many to object, and fortunately the name was retained.

Using resources to manufacture goods for sale has always been a part of life in Alberta.

Medicine Hat is famous for making pottery. The Medalta pots shown here are examples of the jars and jugs produced in the early days of the pottery. The pottery manufacturers wanted to draw attention to their town, Medicine Hat, and their province, Alberta, and created the name Medalta for this purpose. Today these pieces are widely prized and collected.

Medicine Hat, 16" × 20", Oil on Linen, RFM McInnis

N

Nanton

Nanton was named in 1893 for Sir Augustus Nanton. He lived in Winnipeg, but directed the work of Osler, Hammond and Nanton. They owned western Canada's largest financial company at the time. Railways were being built in the 1890s to open up the centre of the area that became Alberta for settlement. The CPR contracted the company to plan townsites along its railway lines. The Calgary and Edmonton Railway was built north to Edmonton, and south almost to the American border. Many towns needing names sprang up almost overnight. At first this little railway stop was called Mosquito Creek, but it soon was renamed to honour Nanton.

Nanton is located very near to Connemara, the home of the artist who painted this scene. We all have a home town. What do you think is special about yours? During our Centennial we can reflect on what makes our home places special.

Nanton, 16" × 20", Oil on Linen, RFM McInnis

O

Onefour

Onefour is an Alberta locality named for a mistake. Early settlers named it because they thought it was located in Township One Range Four. Later surveys showed that it was really located in Township Two Range Four, but by then the name was in use. Although on the map at Township Two Range Four, the name Onefour is still used for this spot, reminding us of this early muddle.

Surveyors marked off the land into townships and ranges to allow settlers to locate and claim land to farm or develop. Soon post offices and school districts were set up. Then names were needed to help people find these places in the plains and mountains.

This painting tells a story. The painter and his wife were out painting when the wind came up, blowing their easels and supplies around. Onefour is located just north of the international border, about a hundred miles south of Medicine Hat.

Onefour, 16" × 20", Oil on Linen, RFM McInnis

P

Peace River

The Peace River is one of the great rivers of Alberta. It takes its name from Peace Point near Lake Athabasca, where Cree and Beaver peoples settled a dispute peacefully. This name has been used for many years.

First Nations people created naming systems that helped them know where they were before any surveys were done in Alberta. Besides naming areas for specific events that occurred in them, geographic features were named for things they resembled. This created shared knowledge of boundaries and places that served as "maps". The Hand Hills, called michichi ispatinan in Cree, are one example. Five ridges radiate from one point, looking like the fingers on a hand.

In this picture the painter views the magnificent Peace River Valley from one of the most popular viewpoints. This lookout high above the river valley is famous as the burial place of "Twelve-foot Davis," a legendary prospector who moved to the area with the riches he gleaned from a claim that was only twelve feet wide.

Peace River, 16" × 20", Oil on Linen, RFM McInnis

Q

Queenstown

In 1888 a Canadian surveyor named Captain Dawson was working in the open plains near this location. He named the site for his native city of Queenstown, Ireland, now known as Cobh. The following year he formed the Canadian Pacific Colonization Company and tried to attract settlers to the area. This always was a hard country to settle and farm. Roads, and later aircraft, finally closed the distances.

Alberta is a province with vast expanses of land. Aircraft have helped farmers to bridge those distances. The cropduster in this painting is used to spray herbicides and pesticides on crops to protect them.

Queenstown, 16" × 20", Oil on Linen, RFM McInnis

R

Redcliff

The name Redcliff is descriptive of the bright red shale cliffs seen along the South Saskatchewan River just south and east of the city. The Canadian Pacific Railway reached this point on its push westward in 1883. Redcliff seems to have been used for years as the name for this locality even before the town grew up there.

Redcliff is located just northwest of Medicine Hat. The communities share a history based on glass and pottery products manufactured at one time in large factories using natural gas. Clay deposits were the basis of the growth of this industry in both cities.

Redcliff, 16" × 20", Oil on Linen, RFM McInnis

S

Sheerness

This scattered little locality found in the middle of the vast open plains was named for a seaport in Kent, England. The post master, George Crozier, first used the name Sheerness in 1910. The post office was closed in 1970.

Today immense strip mines provide the coal which fuels the power generation for our farms and cities. Once Alberta was known as "The Coal Bucket of Canada" because of the huge deposits of coal.

Sheerness, 48" × 60", Oil on Linen, RFM McInnis

T

Turner Valley

Many Alberta place-names are derived from the first settlers who arrived in a district.

Turner Valley was named for Scottish homesteaders Robert and James Turner. They settled on the north fork of Sheep Creek, at the north end of the valley, in 1886. The Turners were noted horse and cattle breeders in the 1880s.

Turner Valley is now most remembered as the place where the first major oil and natural gas discoveries were made in Alberta, although the first oil well was actually drilled at Oil City, in Waterton Lakes National Park, in 1901. This painting shows Turner Valley at the height of natural gas production, with the blazing flares that lit the night sky for years and became synonymous with the area.

Turner Valley, 16" × 20", Oil on Linen, RFM McInnis

U

Bar U Ranch

The Bar U Ranch was one of the largest in western Canada in its day. It was set up in 1882. Today it is a National Historic Site where you can see what ranching was like long ago. The name refers to the brand registered by the ranch.

The Bar U operated as a working ranch from 1882 to 1950. Many influential ranchers were shareholders and managers. Fred Stimson, George Lane, and Patrick Burns all guided the Bar U. John Ware, the famous black cowboy, and Harry Longabaugh, who gained notoriety as the Sundance Kid of outlaw fame, worked here. Now the ranch site is a working museum, a reminder of the "Cowboy Way," a monument to the many people who made, and still make, their life on ranches in Alberta.

Bar U Ranch, 20" × 20", Oil on Linen, RFM McInnis

V

Vulcan

The name Vulcan was first used on the post office in the community when it opened in 1910. For many years the town was known for having the longest line of grain elevators in Alberta.

The ancient Roman god of fire and metalworking, Vulcan, was known by his forge and hammer. Vulcan, on the desolate plains, was forged by the summer heat and tempered by the winter cold, so the name fitted. The streets once were named for mythical beings like Apollo, Venus and Neptune, but later these names were changed.

Today Vulcan has embraced a more recent mythology. People gather here to emulate "Vulcans" from another solar system. The Enterprise and its crew, of Star Trek fame, are celebrated in the town and in this painting.

Vulcan, 16" × 20", Oil on Linen, RFM McInnis

W Writing-On-Stone Provincial Park

The first name for this locality was Masinasin, suggested by a Royal North-West Mounted Police constable posted there. Masinasin is a Cree word meaning "writing on stone." The Blackfoot name is ke-nock-sis-sah-ti. These names refer to the many petroglyphs, or rock carvings, found in the soft sandstone cliffs and hoodoos along the Milk River. Visitors have been amazed and mystified for years by the figures of men and animals, battle scenes and magical beasts to be seen there. When the provincial park was opened in 1957 it was given the English language translation of the Cree name.

Writing-on-Stone Provincial Park, 20" × 20", Oil on Linen, RFM McInnis

X

X marks the spot

Everyone has a place where they live. We all have special places we like to visit.

Do you know where the names of your special places come from?

X marks the spot, 20" × 20", Oil on Linen, RFM McInnis

Y

Yellowhead Pass

Yellowhead Pass is the lowest crossing of the Continental Divide in North America. It was used for years by the First Nations, and found and used by European traders during the 1820s. The fur traders used this route to travel to the west coast.

There have been several stories over the years about how the pass got its name. They involve men named Francois Decoigne, Pierre Hatsinaton and Pierre Bostanais who worked for the early fur companies.

In the early 1800s the Hudson's Bay Company and its rival, the Northwest Company, hired Iroquois men from around Montreal and Cornwall because they were such skilled canoemen, trappers, hunters and guides. Many people of Iroquois descent remain in Alberta today.

Recent research in early fur-trade records indicates that Pierre Bostonais, an Iroquois known as Tête Jaune, or Yellowhead, worked along the upper Peace River as early as 1816.

In 1825 Pierre Bostonais and his brother Baptiste were with the Hudson's Bay Company party that explored a new trade route into the interior of what is now British Columbia. The pass they used became known as Tête Jaune Pass, named for Pierre. Tête Jaune Cache was first used as a name later that year, because "Yellowhead" stored his supplies and furs there.

The Bostonais brothers then lived among the Carrier people near Fort St. James, and in 1827 moved further northeast into the Findlay River country. They were killed there in September by the local people who felt they were trespassing on their lands.

The name Tête Jaune suggests that Yellowhead may have been a Metis man.

Yellowhead Pass, 16" × 20", Oil on Linen, RFM McInnis

Z

Mount Zengel

The woman in this painting is looking for Mount Zengel. It is behind the other peaks in the Victoria Cross Range.

This mountain was named in 1951. It honours Sgt. Raphael Louis Zengel VC MM, an Albertan who joined the 45th Battalion of the Canadian Expeditionary Force to fight during the First World War. Zengel was born in Minnesota, but moved to Rocky Mountain House. He "joined up" in 1915, and in March 1918 took command of his platoon when his officer and sergeant were wounded. He was awarded a Military Medal for his bravery. Later that year he attacked an enemy gun emplacement and captured it, winning the Victoria Cross. Today men like Zengel are honoured in the Victoria Cross Range of mountains located north of Jasper town.

Many of the place-names in this alphabet originate deep in our history, long before Alberta became a province in 1905. Mount Zengel is the most recently named, but other place-names are being added to the map every year.

Mount Zengel, 16" × 20", Oil on Linen, RFM McInnis

Artist

RFM McInnis was born in Saint John, New Brunswick in 1942, studied art at Saint John Vocational School, graduating with a Diploma in Fine and Applied Arts in 1961. He worked as a news reporter for *Evening Times Globe* and *Telegraph Journal* in Saint John prior to studying photography in the Royal Canadian Air Force. After leaving the RCAF in 1966 to become an illustrator for the Federal Department of Transport in Ottawa, he began a series of moves nationally across Canada to promote his career as a painter of the Canadian landscape and as a figure painter in the Maritime tradition, arriving in Alberta in 1978. He now lives with his wife Françoise Cardinal on an original homestead property at Connemara, Alberta, with great hopes of living in St. Boniface (Winnipeg) next, and perhaps Montréal, after that. McInnis worked as a photographer, reporter, and graphic illustrator before turning to art full time in the early 1970s. He has lived and painted in British Columbia, Alberta, Ontario and Québec. These experiences have provided him with the opportunity to get to know the history, the people, the terrain, and the art scene of most of Canada.

During his stay in Calgary in the late 1970s, he was commissioned to do portraits of the leaders of the Progressive Conservative Party which currently hang in the National Headquarters building in Ottawa. After moving to Ottawa in the early 1980s, *Steel and Steam* was published. This was a limited edition "livre d'artiste" containing eight railway-related serigraphs, with text by Pierre Berton, commemorating the 100th anniversary of the CPR's last spike.

McInnis' interest in the small towns and open vistas of the western prairies led him back to Alberta in the late 1980s where he currently resides and paints near Nanton in Southern Alberta. The paintings of Robert McInnis are represented in many corporate, private and public collections throughout Canada.

Acknowledgements

First, I'd like to thank Ken Tingley for suggesting this project, offering me a challenge outside my usual subject matter by having me paint dinosaurs, spacecraft, and Jasper the Bear for a younger audience. Secondly, I'd like to thank John Kurtz, who came to the rescue from Saskatchewan when all our Alberta publishing avenues seemed to dry up. John was my Regina art dealer until his retirement a few years ago, and he had done several books before, notably on Allen Sapp.

Friend and neighbour rancher Bill Dunn must be thanked for posing for the preliminary drawings for the figures in "B", "K", and "U", and his granddaughters Alexandra and Taryn Balsen and their friend Veronica Lowe in "X". The Balsen sisters and their mother Eileen ran the cattle drive (on Connemara Road) in the painting "A". My own granddaughter Emily is seen in "Z". My mother, Girlie McInnis, was visiting from New Brunswick, and I enlisted her to pose with me for a photo for "V". She also posed with my wife Françoise Cardinal, for "W". Françoise in turn posed for the figure in "O", and with her friend, the Québec singer Francine Philie, who was visiting from Montréal, for "L". It was their lifelong dream to canoe together on Lake Louise.

Peter Pocklington commissioned me to paint his portrait many years ago. I used a black and white photo of this painting to do Peter's head in "E". I could not remember the colour of his eyes and every effort to reach Peter by phone failed. They could have been blue.

Pieter Uithuisje of Marker Bear Motorcycle Tours of Nanton brought out his motorcycle to pose for "Y". Yes, his hair is yellow. A photo of one of Bernie Lalonde's and Art Scott's Auctions of Nanton and Stavely was utilized for the painting "G" even though the outdoor auction was nowhere near the site. As illustrators, we do what we have to do to create our imagery. It's the same with "I". A small painting I had done earlier of local Nanton rancher Denny Loree's truck bringing water to his cattle, was used to add interest to the foreground. That's me painting in "P", as well as the fur trader in "E". An historical photo of first premier Rutherford served for his portrait. The skates were added to commemorate the lake in south Edmonton where everybody went for recreation until it was filled in and became a residential development. Lastly, I'd like to thank Fiona Connell, Travelling Exhibitions Coordinator, and the Edmonton Art Gallery for their support by touring the paintings around the province in 2005 and 2006. The paintings will be exhibited for sale at Masters Gallery in Calgary following the tour. RFM McInnis photo by Phillip Groves, Winchester, ON

– *RFM McInnis*

Author

Ken Tingley is an author and historian. Born in Moncton, New Brunswick, he came to Alberta at the age of eight, in the Golden Jubilee year, 1955. After one year in Royalties, Alberta (a place-name now found only on a cairn) his family moved to Edmonton, where he has lived since. While studying history at the University of Alberta, Ken worked on Fort Edmonton Park's 1973 commemoration of the centennial of the North-West Mounted Police. His published works reflect his knowledge of and interest in a wide range of historically important times, events and people in Alberta's past. They include diverse subjects such as the development of large-scale prairie agriculture, in *Steam and Steel: Aspects of Breaking the Land in Alberta*, urban history in *The Best of the Strathcona Plain Dealer*, and the importance of Alberta's military contribution to both world wars, in *For King and Country, Alberta in the Second World War* and *The Path of Duty, The Wartime Letters of Alwyn Bramley-Moore, 1914–1916*. Ken has also written for *Legacy Magazine*, *ATA Magazine*, the *Edmonton Journal*, and *Museums Alberta Review*. One of his most recent projects was completing the text for the official display at Edmonton City hall celebrating Edmonton's Centennial year, 2004.

Ken has contributed to many civic and provincial programs that preserve and protect our shared heritage in Alberta. He has worked to assist in the designation of a number of buildings as historic sites through Community Services. As a member of the Edmonton Historic Resource Inventory Panel he uses his knowledge to assist in evaluating buildings nominated for inclusion on the civic inventory of historically and architecturally significant buildings. He has also lent his considerable expertise and energies to many volunteer organizations, including The Edmonton and District Historical Society, The Old Strathcona Foundation and the Edmonton Historical Board.

His time with two volunteer groups, the national group, Canadian Society for the Study of Names, and its Alberta counterpart, Friends of Geographic Names of Alberta, inspired this book. Ken's work editing publications, making presentations to conferences, and promoting the importance of understanding place-names in schools and in the community, combined with the pleasure of reading the new picture books often brought home by his educator wife, Sheila, provided the impetus for *A is Alberta: A Centennial Alphabet*.

Ken received an achievement award from the Edmonton Historical Board for his work as a local historian. He looks forward to continuing to share his love of Alberta's history with others through volunteer work and writing.

Acknowledgements

My wife Sheila offered tireless support and indispensable suggestions as this project became as special to her as it was for me. Merrily Aubrey, Geographical Names Program Coordinator, for Historic Sites Service of Alberta Community Development, provided valuable information on several sites. David Smythe was of special help in unraveling the various accounts of the naming of Yellowhead Pass through his research, and it was Michael Payne who put me in touch with this valuable material.

The book never could have happened without the wonderful paintings of RFM McInnis, and the enthusiastic support of John Kurtz. Thanks to one and all who supported *A is Alberta*.

– Ken Tingley

Note From The Publisher

John J. Kurtz

Alberta and Saskatchewan are neighbouring provinces, and share birthdays, as they both became provinces in Canada on September 1st, 1905. In September 2004, we published *Happy Centennial Saskatchewan* and we are honoured to present *A is Alberta: A Centennial Alphabet.*

Both the artist and author were born in New Brunswick and answered the call of the West, residing and working in Alberta for many years. What a wonderful way to celebrate Alberta's 100th birthday—combining the beauty in paintings by a noted Alberta artist, RFM McInnis, and the writing talents of a celebrated historian and author, Ken Tingley.

The paintings by RFM McInnis magnify the diverse and spectacular scenery of Alberta, which annually draws thousands of visitors from all over the world, and the descriptive writings by Ken Tingley add historical significance to many places in this province.

Early evidence of human occupation in Bow Valley has been found by archaeologists dating back to 11,000 B.C., and the Plains Indians join with people of different cultures in celebrating Alberta's centennial. The people of Alberta are justifiably proud of their heritage and confidently move forward as they celebrate Centennial 2005.

Further Reading

Alberta Culture and Multiculturalism, Friends of Geographical Names of Alberta Society and University of Calgary Press, *Place Names of Alberta* [four volumes].

Aphrodite Karamitsanis, *Place Names of Alberta, Volume I, Mountains, Mountain Parks and Foothills*. Calgary: Alberta Culture and Multiculturalism, Friends of Geographical Names of Alberta Society and University of Calgary Press, 1991.

Aphrodite Karamitsanis, *Place Names of Alberta, Volume II, Southern Alberta*. Calgary: Alberta Culture and Multiculturalism, Friends of Geographical Names of Alberta Society and University of Calgary Press, 1992.

Tracey Harrison, *Place Names of Alberta, Volume III, Central Alberta*. Calgary: Alberta Culture and Multiculturalism, Friends of Geographical Names of Alberta Society and University of Calgary Press, 1994.

Merrily K. Aubrey, *Place Names of Alberta, Volume IV, Northern Alberta*. Calgary: Alberta Culture and Multiculturalism, Friends of Geographical Names of Alberta Society and University of Calgary Press, 1996.

Don Beers, *The World of Lake Louise A Guide for Hikers*. Calgary: Highline Publishing, 1991.

Marcel M.C. Dirk, *But Names Will Never Hurt Me. Why Medicine Hat? Legends Behind the Naming of the City*. Medicine Hat: Holmes Printing, 1993.

Friends of Geographical Names of Alberta Society, www.albertaplacenames.ca

Simple Truth Publications
2861 23rd Ave.
Regina, SK   S4S1E7

Masters Gallery is pleased to host the launch of *A is Alberta: A Centennial Alphabet.* Masters Gallery will have an exhibition of paintings by RFM McInnis when a present tour of Alberta, organized by the Edmonton Art Gallery, expires.

Printed and bound in Canada by
Friesens, Altona, Manitoba

ISBN 0-9733500-2-4

Dedication
This book is dedicated to the people of Alberta who have contributed time and talent to their province in the past 100 years, and those living today who look forward with confidence and pride to the future.